MAYWEED

Also by Frannie Lindsay

Where She Always Was

Lamb

Mayweed

Frannie Lindsay

Winner of the 2009 Washington Prize

The Word Works
Washington, D.C.

First Edition, First Printing
Mayweed

The WORD WORKS
PO Box 42164
Washington, DC 20015
editor@wordworksdc.com

Cover art from *Prayers and Whispers* by Deborah Mayhall Bradshaw
Author photo by Mary Bonina

Book design by Janice Olson

Printed by Signature Book Printing, Inc.
www.sbpbooks.com

Library of Congress Number: 2009936388
International Standard Book Number: 9780915380732

Acknowledgments

The following poems have appeared or are forthcoming in the following periodicals:

Agni Online: Anubis

Bat City Review: Pet

Black Warrior Review: Shelter

Field: The Urn Garden, Pulling off the Highway on the Way to a Deathbed to Visit a Workhorse at Rest, Sixty

The Georgia Review: Elegy for My Father

Harvard Divinity Bulletin: The Thrift Shop Dresses, Prayer for My Sister

Margie: Imagining My Father as a Child

The Missouri Review (2008 Missouri Review Prize): In Bed with Janet, Vandalizing My Sister's House, Pleasure, The Good Day, Enough, Encore, The Music is Going Great in Both Directions, Ginny

Pebble Lake Review: Disparate Prayer

Poet Lore: The Ghost of an Old Man Sets Down His Beer, Ride, My Father's Haiku

Poetry East: Empty Wheelchair in a Linoleum Hallway

Poetry International: To a Flowering Plum Tree on Beacon Street

Prairie Schooner: Best Friend, Brushing My Father's Hair, Friendship Circle, To the First of September

Salamander: Girlfriends Braiding Each Other's Hair, To My Death, To a Magnolia Tree after a Rainstorm, Keeping a Tropical Plant Alive in the North, To November

Southern Review: Grace

Subtropics: Let me keep some of the dust from home

Valparaiso Poetry Review: Mercies, Prayer on Janet's Birthday, Grandmother of the Groom

The Yale Review: Old Man Swimming

The author acknowledges her debt of gratitude to the following people without whose wisdom and forbearance these poems could not have come into being: John Anderson, Mary Bonina, Ann Killough, Michael Mack, E.B. Moore, Tam Neville, Susan Nisenbaum Becker, Bert Stern, and Christine Tierney.

for Janet

Contents

Moonweed

Mayweed

Rise now from kneeling
in front of your east-facing window
lamenting your sins aloud
to the slugs in your garden. Sunrise is only
a shrine to itself. Consider instead

the fantail fish in the bowl
on your son's cluttered dresser, the peace
of her prettiness. Or your dog,
mutt that he is, asleep in his comfortable fur.
Consider the wind

on the gleaming back of the mother squirrel
dragging a taco shell patiently over
the chain link and up to her spiny nest
pulsing with newborns. No one will ask you
ever again to recite

the dark testaments. Let them rest
on their dour brocades with nothing further
to teach you. You needn't cry
for mercy, or await the right visions
before stumbling home to the village.

Someone will always be singing the hymns
your father loved. The edict of grief has come
to its natural end,
and the wafer dry on your tongue
is the strawberry moon.

Let your shame drowse as snow
in the willow's brittle tresses,
on the meadow grass's deafened tips.
Then let the valley of death flood simply
with mayweed, earnest as milkmaids.

all the leaves will fall on my breast
it will rain on my soul all day all night
my feet will want to march to where you are sleeping
but I shall go on living.

Pablo Neruda,
"The Dead Woman"

Enough

I can almost be happy
remembering my sister's cello
filling our dread-laden house

those November school nights
aglare with algebra homework,
my mother's heavy china

kthunking around in the soapy sink,
the dog my father hated
barking too much

from his far rope length,
hiss of the heat coming on,
and my sister quietly closing

her bedroom door as if she knew
even then she would die
before we did, rosining up

the hand-hewn bow
she hoped would stay
in the family, then folding

her shy body over the curvy wood
like a supplicant
and adjusting the steel endpin

until she was tall with Bach.

Grace

Praise my plain young mother for leaving
her husband's bed at four in the morning
fumbling around for her bifocals
carting her stained velour slippers
down the raw-grained stairs not tying
her robe sliding her violin from between
the magazine rack and the firewood
easing past the mantelpiece scattered
with wedding portraits

praise the caked galoshes drying beside
the basement door swollen away
from its frame and the top step's narrow slat
praise her large bare feet
their tough and knotty bunions
the cool of her hand on her sheet music
praise the scotch tape on the spine
of her Bach and its weakening glue
her penciled maiden name

praise the steadfast ladderback chair
and the music stand there in the basement
the set tubs the damp socks
and undershirts draped too close
to her shoulders praise her shoulders
limber and painless for three brief hours
praise the rosin's glide down her bow
the throaty fifths the sacrament
of her tuning

praise the measure she counted aloud
and the downbeat's breath-lunge
praise her calloused and lovely fingerpads

the noteprints the sixty-watt bulb
the mud-plashed screen through which
the unsorrowing ends of the night slipped in
and although she did not ask to be touched
praise how they lifted up the brittle
wisps of her perm

Elegy for My Father

At last you are small as a boy's
woolen cap in your blue-wrapped box
in the earth,

small as the shovel's first gravelly cough;
and all the slow cars
are gone at last,

and I am thankful for each purple star
that bloomed awhile on the soles of your feet;
for the tears

your body shed in its brief, untroubled sleep;
for your cirrus hair I never wanted
to touch,

between my fingers at last
so like the stone-scented fur of an animal
I am afraid of no longer;

and for the rite of watching death enter and wax
the glow of its lamp inside the hut
of your face, lovely

at last; and at last
for your sweet, infrequent breathing;
and the last teeth

in your mouth; and all the prayers
for nothing; for nothing now
is kind or cruel.

To the First of September

Even the rain is tired of raining
on the white feral cat
heavy again with kittens
lumbering out from behind
the crooked trash bins

and the grass out of breath was convinced
you never would come
oh herald of the right despair
the boxes of dark have started
to pile up on the porch

where the weeds are tired too
of wrapping around themselves
and the small of the bentwood rocker
aches across each reed of its caning

but still I will leave on the light
for your moths and set out a pan
for your first oak petals to collect in
and lock nothing out of pity
for your hoodlum wind

The Thrift Shop Dresses

I slid the white louvers shut so I could stand in your closet
a little while among the throng of flowered dresses
you hadn't worn in years, and touch the creases
on each of their sleeves that smelled of forgiveness
and even though you would still be alive a few more days
I knew they were ready to let themselves be
packed into liquor store boxes simply
because you had asked that of them,
and dropped at the door of the Salvation Army
without having noticed me
wrapping my arms around so many at once
that one slipped a big padded shoulder off of its hanger
as if to return the embrace.

Let me keep some of the dust from home

in my knick-knack tin boxed up
with the scarves and teapot; packed tight

with the rumpled handfuls
of headlines. These are the days when dust

can break, and who else is going to want
this gnarl of hair, this lint from the sisal mat,

this crumb from a biscuit here in my drawer
of ugly things. Let me bring out

my silken dust at each year's snowless dwindling;
and again as May lies down on its weeds in the heat;

and one last time as sleep begins to fall from me
and my legs tangle up in their walking

and the torn shade in the window
of heaven's hut

lifts

To My Old Apartment Key

Oh talisman worth less now
than the carpenter's nail you hung on
those twenty-two years of devout utility
while I lived in the sweet dread of losing you,

on this the day of the changing of locks
as the bold shoes that were never to come
tromp to the middle of the floor that gleams
from the final glide of the amnesia crew,

and the first box is loaded off the red hand truck
as north of all I know
I pay for the scone I don't want
on the long walk to the rattly cross-town bus

and mistake you again
for one of the uneager quarters loose in the dark
of my hand-me-down purse,
oh fugitive from the simplest fumbling,

fear not

The Good Day

Today you are riding your ten-speed,
the bikeway breeze on your cancery breast.
It's a good day, you love

your old Schwinn, the headwind peels
your shirt back, your sparse streamers of hair
fly behind you, your shadow

ravels, your legs rise and float like hawk wings
over the pedals, your fists slacken and lift
from the gears and brakes.

You who grew too small for your loveliness
miles ago, have never been
lovelier. When you close your eyes

you can watch the aspens and cloud rags
race through the valley of death.
Your tires could wobble, happy

forever, over
the dirt and the tough little stones.

The Music Is Going Great in Both Directions

Toward the end her uproarious prattle
which all of the doctors started to call *word salad*
meant nothing at all, but once in a while
she would stop as if she had caught herself
dying and thought it impolite,
and take enough of a sense-starved breath
to say *Lord I'm struggling*
as if that declaration were a fragment
of riverbed rock being pulled loose,
and when she could barely hang on

to a phone but would not let anyone hang it up
she told me I was the nicest cauliflower
she'd ever played, her ravaged voice
pleased as a housewife
pulling her first rhubarb pie from the oven;
then she stopped again
scanning that hazel-skied brain of hers
and she said *the music is going great in both directions*
as if to reassure me, as if to be certain
I'd take that straight to the bank.

To Old Age

All you have left to do
is pull on the splotched cotton gloves you saved for this
turn your freckled back to the library spire and the sunrise

and let them light on your knuckles your shoulders
the transparent bed of your hair
be a ragscape

old woman heavy at last
with the company of pigeons who want nothing more
than to flick the bread and the basement silt

from your palms onto the river littered already
with scraps of daylight
bless your high creased forehead your thrilling patience

open now your Novembered and loverless arms
and let them come
let the filthy and amiable birds all come

To My Death

Thank you for never insisting
on being different from all of the others
that came before you

the peterings the matronly doors
ajar without protest
the white hallways the greatcoats

swaying a little on their hooks
the telephone numbers still connected
while you a world or less away

are without woe
for this is your day of presence it is always
morning the new summer starting

the stars gone back
to the lips of the jump-ups while the initiates
makers of sunrise and cloud shield

gather again for their festival of silence
their spades the instruments of this
meekest baptism

the final tear of soup refused an elixir
the agonal rasp a proclamation
of every name at once thank you

in all your dutiful randomness
for keeping among them
my place

Pet

If my father were only a turtle, I'd keep him
in one of those plastic turtle containers
they sold back then at Woolworth's,
round, with an inch of water,

a kelly green palm tree smack
in the middle. I'd buy him a shaker
of housefly legs, and these I would sprinkle
over the top of his tepid pond.

Once a week I would scoop him up,
plunk him down in the sink to wait
while I rinsed and wiped his lagoon
with ammonia; and all this time

he would jam his head and his legs and his tail
into the handy case of himself
and stay put at the drain's edge,
all the clean knives leaning out

from the rack, and a daisy
stenciled onto his shell.

Anubis

Right after he died, valium-happy
on two dozen milkbones,
eyes open, in the first moment ever
to mean nothing, the dry blue
sash of his tongue flopped
all the way out, ten or so inches
of life-lick gone
dusky. Three biscuit crumbs—
veggie, cheese, poultry—stuck
where the flick of his swallow
had stopped. But I thanked the quiet
vet who had let me help
then I sent him away from the room,
so I could finally
turn off the light to hold
the cold new gift of him, and cradle
his deep chest still gleaming
with fever against my cheek.

Pulling off the Highway on the Way to a Deathbed to Visit a Workhorse at Rest

for Amy Stephens

We are no more
than matter, our hair on the wind off the foothills
will not even be

ash hovered above a collapsing wave
off a coast harsh with gulls;
still, look how

Levi the aged Clydesdale bends his stupendous neck,
his braided mane tangled
with sunlight,

over his mess of hay and oats;
look how his hips, shuddering with arthritis,
are sturdy enough

to walk the corral's perimeter, completely
ignoring us, noble no longer, his gorgeous red hide
flicking nothing away

but heat, his fine pale fetlocks muddied
by urine and dirt,
his hooves

that worked the acres when we were young
imbedded with pebbles. And still, look
how his venerable, achy legs,

hour by rainless hour,
with all the gravity once entrusted to them, now
stamp only the dust by his water pail.

To the Last Saturday in October

While you are still here,
I know you will forgive me
this one last time

if I can't heed
your shallow prayer
in the rapids, its nattering on
to God-lit simplicity,

if I ignore your dimming
that visits too early
these bright bare woods;

forgive me this once
if I listen instead to the word
the stiffened grass might
make itself say

if I press a brown reed of it—
one shrill, dying reed—
in my cupped hands'

cracked ocarina
where the sparrow I found
still alive this morning

belongs: its drying note,
its pebble of lyric,
the whistle you tried so hard
to teach me

I'm like a rifle that's a little out of date
but very accurate: when I love
there's a strong recoil, back to childhood, and it hurts.

Yehuda Amichai,
"When I Have a Stomachache"

Friendship Circle

I remember the whole Girl Scout pledge
the handshake the two-finger salute
the circle we formed at the end
of our purposeful meetings there in the echoey gym
by crossing our arms over our stomachs
and joining hands even with Freya who already had
her period singing before we went home
Make New Friends in a round wanting nothing
except our rides our suppers our favorite shows but
squeezing the palm of the girl to the right
passing around the sacred gossip
until it came back as a nervous
boy's fingers the first time inside a blouse
but tonight all of our living mothers
are waiting again for us in the parking lot
by the frozen track field listen
they have cranked their radios low
in the idling light each one of them
wearing the scratchy and crooked scarf
it has taken us weeks and weeks to knit.

Girlfriends Braiding Each Other's Hair

for Chip

But now they are safe: one seated
before the slender and dutiful other,
the ivory handled mirror that has stayed
in her family glass-up on the rug; the sunlight
finding its own temporal girlishness,
while one brushes her best friend's

sacrum-length hair, lifts a swath at a time of it
into her palm and untangles it first
without pulling; then strokes it
from root to end with the boar bristles,
weaving it in, and does the same
with the next and the third

although they were fighting
and crying an hour ago over a boy,
over who had turned in the best
essay on freedom. They have reached this
feminine peace and their faces
are faces of women

they will be in good time, the women
who always did this in the end:
not only two but a circle of women
taking their seats, not facing each other.

Shelter

It was only a joke: her two big sisters
mailing the note to her they had managed to type
on their father's Remington Rand, saying
the Russians are going to bomb
your bedroom today, signed "The Russians"
and telling her she would be safe
if she took off her clothes and went to the attic
alone with no food or juice
just Davey, her stuffed cocker spaniel,
and hid all day in the crease of the folded cot;
so she and the toy dog stayed in that hot, woody dark,
the blue ticked mattress and springs holding them close
like a cloth-and-wire angel, the feathery moths
sipping the sweat on her neck and toes.
When they sounded the all-clear triangle
they had snuck home from the first-grade
orchestra, and stamped up the slivery stairs
loud as police, she cried, but only a little, glad
that the Russians had had a change
of heart, and dropped the bomb
next door, killing just the McLaughlins'
poor noisy parakeet, that they
were her sisters, only her sisters,
who loved her, and that she could smell
the hot shepherd's pie from the kitchen
as they gave her back her white undies
and tee-shirt and corduroy overalls,
as they helped her braid her hair.

In Bed with Janet

Nothing was left for me but the gingerly climb
over the side rails, parting the sheets and arranging
the pillow she gave me to place on her stomach,
all this through the weatherless haze of her morphine drip,
so we could lie together, child to child,
sister to mother and everything wearily
vice versa, and hold her and stroke her hair
gone silky with illness and let her touch me
all over, the cello-bowing hand that had lost its deftness
drooping across my breast and she asked me
is this okay, is anything I am doing
bothering you, and I wanted to say
it was fine, her hand drained of its will
across my breast was fine,

but I moved her wrist
away, her palm an exhausted swimmer
dragging itself onto a steep little island of health
placed back in the deep lake of icy bedclothes,
and she said she was sorry, my dying sister
apologized for that tender, delirious gesture,
so purely lustless and seeking, oh how I wanted to
put her twitching palm over my nipple again,
unsay my refusal and let her hold me,
summon whatever solace she needed from me
like milk, like simple milk.

Prayer on Janet's Birthday

Let the gloves the world needed to touch you
fall away as the last parched leaves
from the birch by the old lake shore
so the waves in the cove
where we waded at night
might exhale once more
over the smooth, unimportant pebbles
and the cattails' unbending stalks,
and the skittish minnows might gleam anew
beneath the moon's godly indifference;
let our dear gray boat hold us deep in its palms
so our damp hair might tangle again
in listless pleasure, so our fig-brown lips
might grow sweet with womanly dark,
and my hand find rest at last
on the wing of the nightgown
I begged you to wear all those years,
o child who lived so long.

Encore

On the first summer night of your death
I fill the kitchen with amateur cello music,

our Gables Retirement Home recital
captured on warbly Radio Shack cassette,

out of tune, all heart, and I am embarrassed
by your raspy tone, afraid that the elderly

lab mix next door will gain back his hearing
just for the high notes

your out-of-practice fingers seem especially fond of
missing, but at the end of the *Ave Maria*

the seventeen drowsy oldsters become exultant
with feathery bravos and so we do it again,

my sister, we do it again

Ginny

When it simply came time for her to stop knowing
what a piano was, or the reason for socks

or kettles, her husband sat her down
in the paisley chair that had stayed in the family

after his own mother died, covered her knees
with the afghan she knit him one year for Christmas,

and told her again how pretty she looked
and rubbed her dry little hands.

And once in a while she gestured, as though
she may have wanted to

stitch or color—the harmless afterflames of intended
motion—anything using her fingers to keep herself

from feeling the Debussy slip from them, as evening
crossed the lawn they had kept together.

As if she were trying to ask him to guide her
outside, quick, before dark,

and help her
bring the white impatiens in.

Grandmother of the Groom

She gets to keep the firefly
that rests on the back of her hand,

and the rose that flops from the bow
on her good white blouse,

freshwater pearl hatpin and all.
And if someone would only

write them down
on a napkin, the names of the boys

who kiss her cheek on their way
to the dance floor.

Best Friend

it wasn't him shoving me against his mother's
nice red house between her swollen
lilacs and squash buds
not his hands or the driveway dirt
and the skinny-boy sweat on them
freezing my shoulders red
in the boiled-to-nothing noon
not his grip so tight I dropped
my girl scout doll face down on the beds
of melon vines not his saying *don't tell don't you*
dare ever tell but his tongue
not a boy's tongue now pushing
my lips apart not for fun
his cherry-red tongue still tasting
of popsicle me not trying

    to hit him yank
at his fingers break a few grab at
his glistening bangs his Roy Rogers belt
whatever I could and twist him
away from the world while I fell
and got up and fell and got up then
took off next door where someone anyone
might be home to let me in stop
reading their book stop
drying their dishes get off the phone
send the other kids upstairs stop telling me *this*
is nothing and help me
comb the terrible knots from my hair

My Father's Haiku

I remember my father in tears
in front of his steep black typewriter

up for hours after his wife had gone
to bed and the shade of his gooseneck

hot as a gridiron
he banged out one haiku after another

jamming the keys until he got them
exactly right

each on a separate sheet of Corrasable Bond
that he later cut up into squares

and taped to 3x5 cards that he kept
in a metal box beside the succotash can

of pencils emery boards
his good fountain pen

I remember finding the one about
his little girl's cigarette butts

in his ashtray
the one about wanting to marry her

off

Unction

Not comb
her broken hair

not curse
not want

not sponge her brow
not drape her bone by bone

not ask
not ache

not pull
her sweatshirt sleeves

over those
veiny blue wrists

not hope
not lie
not keep

not warm the broth
back up

not rage
not rue

not tilt her cup
not read aloud

not elegy
not sin

Pleasure

Toward the end they could not feed my sister
enough, she who had subsisted
on millet and steam-distilled water

let herself wolf down everything under the sun:
waffles and syrup, cashews,
the hospice's cardboardy chocolate mousse.

She let them shampoo and French-braid her hair,
suffered the irises, sunflowers, lilacs
all bearing down from their vases at once,

showed me her left breast hard as a burlap sack
full of barley, asked if I wanted to
touch it, invited me

into the single bed she would die in, kissed me
full on the lips with her failing unfailing
love, slept with a teaspoon

upside down on her tongue so she could keep on
making saliva, but really because
it felt good. It just felt good.

Vandalizing My Sister's House

When I knew she was not coming back, I lay down
for a nap on the coarse sheets my sister had left

on her sickbed; fiddled around with the knee crank
and head crank; snooped through her bureau and

hocked her best panties; finished her
Easter egg-shaped m&ms; poured the last of her

store-brand shampoo down the sink; drank straight
from her opened carton of juice; spilled her pills

onto the dining room table: the pink antipsychotics,
spring-yellow valium, the speckled morphine;

opened her windows that terrible night, opened
all of them wide; misplaced her house keys

and did not stay sorry; just kept busy helping
the good dark let itself in.

Not yesterday I learned to know
The love of bare November days
Before the coming of the snow,
But it were vain to tell her so,
And they were better for her praise.

Robert Frost,
"My November Guest"

Dusk

Leave dusk alone with the dog
whose lungs fail
to flood with voice and eagerness,
whose slowed walks home

leave paw-gasps on the lawn;
with the ragged plume of tail
the harried wind has no time left
to riffle in its goings away;

amid the dandruff flakes
that clutter the tumbling fur;
along the cracked gray slope of nose
that tastes of mulch and poverty;

with each knot in the patient leash
on the mudroom hook
and on the human lips that whistle less; alone
within the cool and waxen ears that crane

to hear their summon from the stairs.
Leave dusk upon the mist that dims
the kick-dreams and the instincts low
inside the kindly brain; and deep

beneath the emerald ice of cataracts
for dusk alone
knows crusted eyes need peace,
and time now with their dark.

To November

Here you come before we have had any time
to take our solemn coats our hats that itch back out
of the naphthalene dark   you glide as though you believed
our gusty scarves and the flags of our breath
were welcoming you   here you come with nothing
to love except your own vibrant bleakness

sweeping the birds with your few stern strokes of hay
wide is your intent on songlessness
oh husher of all that has ever beseeched
oh nearsighted pipe-metal noon
puller of smoke from the unready chimneys
are you not at once reluctance and hastened departure

with nowhere to go except every north-facing stoop
each complaining screen door in which a tired wife
has just given up waiting   I offer you this
lashed bundle of all that is still
too damp to burn

Disparate Prayer

Go away from the kingdom of earth
where you loved me

follow the ground mist's weave
that leads to the boathouse
where all the red kayaks rock without solace

keep going do not rest there
keep going my precious companion

beneath the remorseless starlight
that leaves each narrow street to its whistling
go and do not call my name

for the last few brown paper tongues
of the sycamore outside our window

rattle now only in elegy
and cannot send word

keep going until your shadow's fingers
rip on each ice-burnt twig

and the first wrens back
carry the husks of them up
to seal their nests from the spring wind

that is harshest along the river's far bank
where you are found
kneeling at last

To the Flowering Plum Tree on Beacon Street

And here you are
outside the Sovereign Bank

in the night-blown rain, old now; almost unable
to grip your million blossoms,

bride whose groom, spring after blustery spring,
doesn't show up;

what can you do
but stand there, idly fashion one more

sapwood ring of your own, and keep on
sighing

Visiting Hours

Sometimes he tried to crank his bed by himself,
and his baby blue snowflaked gown would ride up
and there was his drowsy penis that meant nothing to him,
his thigh skin gathered like prom gown taffeta.
He just kept gabbing away: how tired he was
of Bach, the detective books he was starting
to not understand, what he had eaten
for breakfast, and now and again
he would stop and call Marisol in
to hoist him onto the bedside commode
so he could try to move his mulish bowels
for the first time all week, and afterwards
she would slide on her gloves and clean him
and he would go back to his nattering, this dying man
who had not been ashamed for a single hour of his life,
not after he struck his daughter when she was afraid
so that she would have something to fear, not after
he lifted her buttercup nighty over her legs
on the hottest nights of the summer
when she was a girl kept small
by her unfettered need of him, a girl
who adored the sound of his baritone voice.
And not now.

Keeping a Tropical Plant Alive in the North

In the shade of your dying, all things
tend themselves:
six huge boys lope home from detention;

the same woman draped in her backwards coat
falls asleep on the 86 bus;
northern birds flood the old, stony sky.

The worlds that need to end today
are ending. What else
can I do for you:

pinch off your just-browned leaves, turn
the side you tilt toward me
back into the light.

Imagining My Father as a Child

Only then could I slide my hands
along his meager biceps under the shirt
he'd slept in; stroke the back of his neck;
and press my finger pads
to the coin-sized moles on his scalp,
the last threads of his hair beneath
my circling thumbs; and strum his face
from which the hate had gleamed:

the crippled brows still black,
the tearless eyes, the bright webs
straining another day's worth of blood
to his cheeks. I rubbed and did not stop,
and I want to say that the watchful
hum of the lights in his room
fell silent, or that the peace
was small enough to keep us both;

or that, at least, a starling
lit outside the window
to pick at the frozen earth,
but it did not.

Ride

I did not ask, but knelt, unlocked the wheels
of his chair so it would coast, a tour boat
over the linoleum, past
the nurses' backs and out beyond
the sign-in book and dish of mints,
the lurching doors, out farther, down
the frost-heaved walk, the pocked,
maternal sycamores. He wanted nothing

of the world he'd not seen
for two years, nothing but the stout will
not to leave it, not to pass yet
through the crooked gate in need
of paint, the yellow lab behind it barking,
barking at her slimy tennis ball lodged tight
beneath a spindly lilac bush; the grass brown
from the overtired sun, one purple crocus up.

Mercies

Blue leather slippers under his bed;
cup full of licorice; ice chips in a pitcher;
daughter, grown thin, still propping his head;

large-print novels, his wedding picture;
the African violet his nurse meant to water;
postcards sent every week of the winter;

the days he crossed off in red magic marker:
April. May. Now June's bored wind
runs out of paper:

day book—the French masters—
closed on his dresser.

Brushing My Father's Hair

I brushed his hair the wrong way
but I brushed it,

rummaged and found the doll-small brush
in the second drawer down while he slept

sitting up; I worked
the strands in an eye-of-the-hurricane

whirl, and kept quiet inside the quiet
of being a daughter, counting

to fifty, then the next fifty, the brush's
breath-sounds no longer

counting; then I patted the jagged
sideburns, curled the nape hairs

around his ears sprouting
delicate, wretched tufts of their own,

and I spat on my palm
and flattened the cowlick,

so he would look nice.

Empty Wheelchair in a Linoleum Hallway

And all at once I know where you are
although there is no light yet

through the tear in my shade, only
the ease of my waking after

your death's short night; and the touch
of the rain on my coat as I walk my dog

around the dozy block;

as the school buses wheeze again
and empty of all their clattering colors;

as none of this hopes
to be cherished; nor all the fears

you left; nor the shrill and foolish beaks
of the honeysuckle cramming

into the breeze.

To a Black Cat on an April Morning

I believe
in your unrelenting neutrality

in the sheen of your muscles
flashing the code of its heedless mirror

at the ending world
as you yawn your way along the ridge

of your clovery abyss, boding
nothing, flicking your tail's

unasking signals—

and I believe
in the lesser silences—

one stark morning further away
from death—

the gleam of the doubting
sun on the drainpipe—

how the prickly gray blossoms, nervous
familiars,

let the wind, fumbling into its old
prayer gloves,

stroke them—

The Urn Garden

They slid you free of the hearse
in a cardboard box shaped just like the boxes
florists use for their lanky roses,

but this box big as a man
with a night-green wreath where the face
belongs. I came because

I needed to know the right father
had died; to cast the borrowed coat
of my mercy down.

You took an afternoon to die, another
afternoon to burn. Both,
I stayed with you.

I might have shopped, or wept, or practiced naming
the rowdy morning birds by their calls
but I sat instead in the chapel,

made lists on some Kleenex,
then slipped loose at last
of your vast cold sleeves,

and wandered the young summer day
bare-armed, heavy with life,
a daughter no longer.

Sixty

When my foremothers' bureaus
have cluttered themselves

with the outsized brooches
that clawed the hearts of sweaters

long since given away,
when my hair cannot keep

from telling its raspy testament
to the whole of the winter air,

when starlight has come to know
for all its dimes' worth of weightlessness

that it can do nothing,
and not even quiet is simple,

then let me lift the sack cloth
from every mirror and draw close

and take pity on each of
my neck's old erogenous furrows,

then, merely because
the dutiful, matronly sun has come back,

let me fling wide the door
on the boisterous garden of death.

The Ghost of an Old Man Sets Down His Beer

Now from the porch at dusk my father can reach
as far as the pavement's end and touch the doe's ear

just before she looks up and shambles away
from the weed tuft she has been nibbling

back to her fawn in a blueberry patch
year by year she has come to know as a neighbor might

his Chevy's lumbering over the pebbles
down to his cottage on the quiet side of the lake

Old Man Swimming

The one time he was purely happy
was when he lay himself down in the water

backfloating tilting his big square chin toward the sun

opening his eyes just enough
when he needed to see where the lake
had taken him flutter-kicking now and again

as he would in time teach me to do
by leaning me backwards

into the childish waves that lapped the dock

and I think he would sometimes nap a little
in the dragonflies' threatless whir

for once going nowhere just letting himself
be carried along atop the slicks
of boat oil and lolling weeds

this old professor hollowed for now
of spite of drunkenness

with the sun's sleep doing the rocking for him
pausing in neither judgment nor grace

in the lake's black hammock

Homecoming

All in good time, I'll go back to walk
the manmade pond's muddy circumference
behind the Broomfield County Hospice
alone, as I did after lunch that June day before
Janet died, everyone else too reluctant
to leave her sickroom's sweltering comfort;

I'll swing that groaning exit door wide
and traverse once more
the shadeless road that bore her away,
and there on the sage-littered shore
the very same heron, stilts high-wading
the coppery shallows,
will have come back too.

To August

The honeysuckle is all but gone,
just a few doll fingers drooping beneath the quiet
weight of one bee;

why have you done it again, learned nothing,
decked yourself out with too many cumbersome stars;
why are you losing your feel

for the green of the rivers,
the succulent early raspberries; your ear for the frond-laden
thunking of bullfrogs at evening;

now nothing fits in your hand, and soon your heart
must be crushed into silt again;
oh scare-dove, hard is the clay of your breast,

and dreadful now are your chills
when they come, and empty now is the shawl of the willow
trailing the dory

and warm
with all the slow fish of your lengthened nights
is the water

Prayer for My Sister

May you rise from the earth as a mulberry tree
in spring, a little away from the cabin road,

may the eager wings of your leaves
shiver daintily in the warming snowlight,

may your strife be redeemed as a vixen
free of her rusted trap, limping home
to her hungry kits,

and your dread of God
as a storm cloud heavy with yes,

and your fine, tired hair
as the slim-throated calls of the peepers
at evening,

and your last travail
as the papery buds that flee from April's gusts,

and your regret as the grief-black fruit
whose sugared inks brighten the beaks
of the fledgling crows,

and the pain that tore your bones
as sunlight calm on the moss-crowned rocks,

and your death as the syllable of mist
on a doe's mouth

at daybreak, safe
from even the weak sun's aim.

Afterword

To a Magnolia Tree after a Rainstorm

You forget how you cried every day
for the ache of the dray horse
hauling the bread wagon

and now your old gust of angst is back
for the street-cleaning truck
for the frowsy women in bathrobes

lifting the rust-gnawed trash can lids
for the reluctant child in her knee socks
and Catholic plaid

you have refused
the rain's impersonal comfort
the unlovely cajoling jays

instead you are sorry for everything
blessed then are all your regrets
blessed your tattered hankies

and blessed, blessed
the twigs of your fingers
without them

About the Washington Prize

Mayweed is the winner of the 2009 Word Works Washington Prize. Frannie Lindsay's manuscript was selected from among 242 manuscripts submitted by American poets.

First Readers:

Stuart Bartow • Michelle Galo • Carol Graser • Elaine Handley
Marilyn McCabe • Kathleen McCoy • Mary Sanders Shartle

Second Readers:

George Drew • Naton Leslie • Jay Rogoff

Final Judges:

Karren Alenier • J. H. Beall • Barbara Ungar
Nancy White • Maria van Beuren

Other Available Washington Prize Books

Ace, Richard Carr
biography of water, Carrie Bennett
Call from Paris, Prartho Sereno
The Cutoff, Jay Rogoff
A Diamond Is Hard But Not Tough, Ann Rae Jonas
Fleur Carnivore, Richard Lyons
Following Fred Astaire, Nathalie F. Anderson
The Hat City after Men Stopped Wearing Hats, John Surowiecki
Last Heat, Peter Blair
One Hundred Children Waiting for a Train, Michael Atkinson
Phoenix Suites, Miles Waggener
Stalking the Florida Panther, Enid Shomer
Sun, Moon, Salt, Nancy White
Survivable World, Ron Mohring
Tipping Point, Fred Marchant

About The Word Works

The Word Works, a nonprofit literary organization, publishes contemporary poetry in collectors' editions. Since 1981, the organization has sponsored the Washington Prize, a $1,500 award to an American poet. Monthly, The Word Works presents free literary programs in the Chevy Chase, MD, Café Muse series, and each summer, free poetry programs are held at the historic Joaquin Miller Cabin in Washington, DC's Rock Creek Park. Annually, two high school students debut in the Miller Cabin Series as winners of the Jacklyn Potter Young Poets Competition.

Since 1974, Word Works programs have included: "In the Shadow of the Capitol," a symposium and archival project on the African-American intellectual community in segregated Washington, DC; the Gunston Arts Center Poetry Series (Ai, Carolyn Forché, and Stanley Kunitz, among others); the Poet-Editor panel discussions at the Writer's Center (John Hollander, Maurice English, Anthony Hecht, Josephine Jacobsen, and others); and Master Class workshops (Agha Shahid Ali, Thomas Lux, Marilyn Nelson).

In 2010, The Word Works will have published 70 titles, including past work from such authors as Deirdra Baldwin, J.H. Beall, Christopher Bursk, John Pauker, Edward Weismiller, and Mac Wellman. Currently, The Word Works publishes books and occasional anthologies under three imprints: the Washington Prize, the Hilary Tham Capital Collection, and International Editions. Information on Toad Hall Editions, a publishing division of The Word Works, can be seen at ToadHallMedia.com.

Past grants to The Word Works have been awarded by the National Endowment for the Arts, National Endowment for the Humanities, DC Commission on the Arts & Humanities, Witter Bynner Foundation, Writer's Center, Bell Atlantic, Batir Foundation, and others, including many generous private patrons.

The Word Works has established an archive of artistic and administrative materials in the Washington Writing Archive housed in the George Washington University Gelman Library.

The Word Works PO Box 42164 Washington, DC 20015
editor@wordworksdc.com www.wordworksdc.com

Other Word Works Books

Hilary Tham Capital Collection

Mel Belin, *Flesh That Was Chrysalis*
Doris Brody, *Judging the Distance*
Sarah Browning, *Whiskey in the Garden of Eden*
Christopher Conlon, *Gilbert and Garbo in Love*
Christopher Conlon, *Mary Falls: Requiem for Mrs. Surratt*
Donna Denizé, *Broken Like Job*
James Hopkins, *Eight Pale Women*
Brandon Johnson, *Love's Skin*
Judith McCombs, *The Habit of Fire*
Kathi Morrison-Taylor, *By the Nest*
Miles David Moore, *The Bears of Paris*
Miles David Moore, *Rollercoaster*
Maria Terrone, *The Bodies We Were Loaned*
Hilary Tham, *Bad Names for Women*
Hilary Tham, *Counting*
Jonathan Vaile, *Blue Cowboy*
Rosemary Winslow, *Green Bodies*

International Editions

James C. Hopkins & Yoko Danno, *The Blue Door*
Moshe Dor, Barbara Goldberg, Giora Leshem, eds., *The Stones Remember*
Myong-Hee Kim, *Crow's Eye View: The Infamy of Lee Sang, Korean Poet*
Vladimir Levchev, *Black Book of the Endangered Species*

Additional Titles

Karren L. Alenier, Hilary Tham, Miles David Moore, eds., *Winners: A Retrospective of the Washington Prize*

Jacklyn Potter, Dwaine Rieves, Gary Stein, eds. *Cabin Fever: Poets at Joaquin Miller's Cabin*

Robert Sargent, *Aspects of a Southern Story*

Robert Sargent, *A Woman From Memphis*

About the Cover Art

Deborah Mayhall Bradshaw lives, designs, and paints from a lyrical log home handcrafted by her husband, Tom, in the high country of western North Carolina. She owns and operates Dancingfish Press, which she created to provide a voice for artists. The press has produced five museum-quality books: *Wayne Trapp, The Journey of a Sculptor; Robert F. Irwin: Forty Years; The Art of Lillian Athey Turchin: An Abundance of Joy; The Private Diary of Noyes Capehart;* and the latest release, *Emily & Me: Poems by Emily Dickinson with Faces by Ellen Beinhorn.*

The paintings from which the cover images for this book were selected are from her original series, *Prayers and Whispers,* an ongoing search for the place where images become prayers.

This book is computer typeset in Centaur. Centaur™ is probably the best known re-creation of the roman type cut by Nicolas Jenson in the fifteenth century. New York's Metropolitan Museum of Art commissioned American typographer Bruce Rogers to design an exclusive type in 1914. It was named Centaur after the title of the first book designed by Rogers using this type: *The Centaur* by Maurice de Guérin, published in 1915. The typeface's companion italics as drawn by Frederic Wade in 1925 are based on the letterforms of sixteenth-century calligrapher Ludovico degli Arrighi. The current digital version of Centaur has both roman and italic, and includes bold weights, small caps, alternates, and swashes.